Henry's House

Creepy-Crawlies

Philip Ardagh

illustrated by Mike Gordon

SCHOLASTIC

For Freddie, again!
P.A.

Consultant: Peter Smithers, entomologist,
University of Plymouth

Editorial Director: Lisa Edwards
Senior Editor: Jill Sawyer

Scholastic Children's Books,
Euston House, 24 Eversholt Street,
London NW1 1DB, UK
a division of Scholastic Ltd
London ~ New York ~ Toronto ~ Sydney ~ Auckland
Mexico City ~ New Delhi ~ Hong Kong

First published in the UK by Scholastic Ltd, 2009

ISBN 978 1407 10718 9

Printed and bound by Tien Wah Press Pte. Ltd, Singapore

10 9 8 7 6 5 4 3 2

Philip Ardagh and Mike Gordon are regular visitors to Henry's House. Philip (the one with the beard) keeps a note of everything that's going on, and even reads a mind or two. Mike (the one without the beard) sketches whatever he sees, however fantastical it may be ... and together they bring you the adventures of Henry, an ordinary boy in an extraordinary house!

Contents

Welcome to Henry's House!

5

Catching the bug

There are lots of different kinds of creepy-crawly. Most are members of three main groups: insects, arachnids and myriapods. There are many different kinds of creepy-crawly in each group.

This is a bug. A bug is a kind of insect. All insects have three main body parts and six legs.

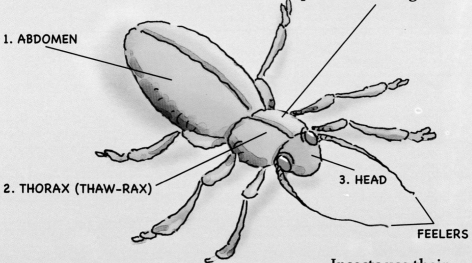

1. ABDOMEN

2. THORAX (THAW-RAX)

3. HEAD

FEELERS

Insects use their feelers for smelling, touching and tasting.

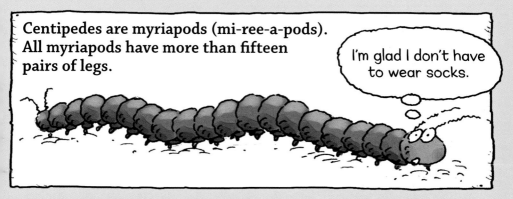

Centipedes are myriapods (mi-ree-a-pods). All myriapods have more than fifteen pairs of legs.

I'm glad I don't have to wear socks.

8

Spiders are arachnids (a-rack-nids). They only have two body parts and eight legs. Insects only have six.

1. CEPHALOTHORAX (SEFF-ALLO-THAW-RAX)

2. ABDOMEN

Spiders don't see better than humans, although most of them have eight eyes.

And I'm short-sighted...

Woodlice are another kind of creepy-crawly called crustacea (crust-ay-sha).

Crabs and lobsters are crustacea too.

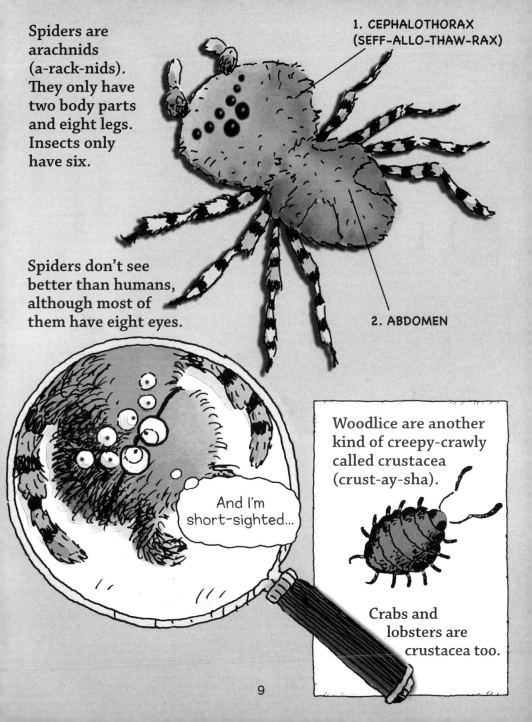

A bug's-eye view

This long-horned grasshopper hears through its legs!

LONG-HORNED GRASSHOPPER

These insects get their names from their long feelers.

LONGHORN BEETLE

Flight, flies and fluttering

An hour later...

You can sleep here, next to Mothball.

BUZZZZZZZZZZZ

None of us is going to sleep with these flies buzzing around!

True flies only have two wings.

BUZZZZZZZZZZZ

My cousin Bruce, a horsefly, can travel at 90 mph (145 kph)!

BUZZZZZZZZZZ

That's me, folks! Tee-hee!

A housefly carries about 2.5 million germs!

DROOL!

Flies cover their food with spit.

Mmmm!

The spit makes it mushy.

Lovely!

SLURP!

Then they suck it up.

Many different types of insect can fly.

A dragonfly is an insect but it isn't a true fly. It has four wings, not two.

I'm not really a dragon, either.

HEAD

1

2

3

4

THORAX

ABDOMEN

A ladybird has four wings.

A butterfly also has four wings, so it isn't a true fly.

Let's try to get some sleep now that those buzzy flies seem to have dozed off.

Wasps!

The next morning...

If you're interested in insects, I suggest we start at the top of the house.

Why, what's up there?

A wasps' nest!

There are about 17,000 different types of wasp.

SEE-THROUGH WINGS

These black-and-yellow stripes mean DANGER.

STINGER

A wasp can use its stinger to sting again and again. Bees can only sting once, then they die.

The potter wasp makes tiny pots from wet clay and lays an egg in each one. Before sealing the top of the pot, she adds a live caterpillar. When the baby wasp hatches, it'll eat the caterpillar as its first meal!

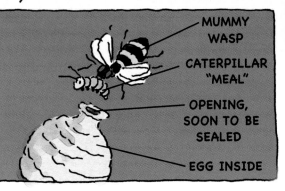

MUMMY WASP

CATERPILLAR "MEAL"

OPENING, SOON TO BE SEALED

EGG INSIDE

The bee's knees!

16

Left alone, honeybees make their nests in trees or gaps in rocks.

The bees make lots of cells from a kind of wax.

CELLS

These cells have been sealed shut.

These cells have honey in them.

The queen bee lays eggs in some of the cells.

I like the beekeeper's outfit!

Beekeepers set up ready-made hives for honeybees to move into.

A family of bees in a hive is called a colony.

That hive looks a bit like my kennel!

Worker bees store pollen in "baskets" on their two back legs.

They brush the pollen into the baskets with their hairy middle legs.

They use their front legs to comb their feelers clean.

FEELERS

POLLEN "BASKET"

Webs worldwide

Why do spiders spin webs?

A spider's web is its home, food-catcher and food store.

MUNCH!

The web is sticky.

When an insect gets stuck in a web the spider gives it a poisonous bite.

The spider wraps the insect in silk. Inside the silk, the poison turns the insect to mush so that the spider can drink it later!

There are three main kinds of web:

ORB WEB

SHEET WEB

TANGLE WEB

For catching flying insects, it's made by garden spiders.

Spun near the ground to catch crawling insects.

Often in the corner of rooms, made by house spiders.

MANDY MUFFET'S SPIDERIFIC FACTS

- The first spiders spun their webs around 400 million years ago.

- Some spiders have their webs all to themselves. Others share. Some webs contain up to 20,000 spiders each!!!

- Some spiders steal the food from other spiders' webs.

- You could make a million spiders' webs from just one teaspoon of silk!

- A black widow spider's poison is FIFTEEN times more deadly than a rattlesnake's.

Little Miss Muffet from the nursery rhyme was a real person. She was the daughter of spider-expert the Reverend Thomas Muffet.

I wonder if that's a tuffet she's sitting on?

Spiders' skeletons are on the outside. As they grow bigger they grow a new skeleton.

I don't have a bone in my body!

SPIDER'S SHED SKIN

Then they shed their old skin. This is called moulting.

Stop staring! I'm getting undressed!

SPIDER IN NEW SKIN

Mmm! Lunch!

Moulting is a dangerous time for spiders. They can't run away or defend themselves against attack.

23

Flutter by, butterflies!

Hi, Big Bug! I wondered where you'd got to.

Who have you got there?

My mate, Eric.

WOW! It's an enormous caterpillar. It must have eaten some of Magnus Boffin's "super-grow" plant food too.

All butterflies and moths start out as eggs and then caterpillars.

Eric has strong jaws for chomping leaves.

These markings are a warning. They mean: "I don't taste nice!"

Eric's tail-end is made to look like his head, to confuse his enemies.

He'll keep these six legs when he becomes a butterfly.

Caterpillars come in all shapes and sizes.

Some butterflies can lay over 50,000 eggs in a lifetime.

The eggs hatch into caterpillars.

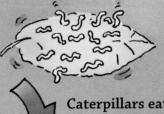

Caterpillars eat many times their own body weight.

As they get bigger, they shed their skin a few times.

When the butterfly finally comes out, its wings are crumpled and soggy.

CHRYSALIS

Inside, the caterpillar begins to turn into a butterfly.

The caterpillar makes a hard case around itself.

A butterfly often rests with its wings shut, the upper sides touching.

Moths rest with their wings open and down, clearly showing the top sides.

TOP SIDE OF WING

UNDERSIDE OF WING

Butterflies and moths have something called a proboscis. They use it like a long drinking straw for getting to the nectar in flowers.

A moth's feelers have little bobbles at the end (and often look feathery).

Ants!

TEE! HEE!
Ants in the ear are
even more tickly than a
moth on the nose!

Ants live in colonies,
often underground.

Different ants in a colony
do different jobs.

These worker ants are
searching for food for
themselves, their queen
and the soldier ants
who guard the colony.

A tasty fact here!

The paper's not bad either.

Food on tap!
Some ant colonies keep aphids (such as greenfly) and "milk" them. They squeeze out sweet liquid to drink!

Some ants can lift 50 times their own weight.

I'm not going to try to save those dog biscuits. Some ants can STING!

A young queen ant has wings. When she is ready to lay eggs in her nest, she doesn't need her wings any more. So she bites them off!

Leafcutter ants eat fungus that grows on leaves in their nest.

Their workers cut out and carry the leaves in pieces to the nest.

The antlion digs a pit in sandy soil then hides at the bottom.

UNSUSPECTING ANT

SNEAKY ANTLION

When an ant slips down the side, the antlion flicks sand at it.

Then it catches the ant in its jaws.

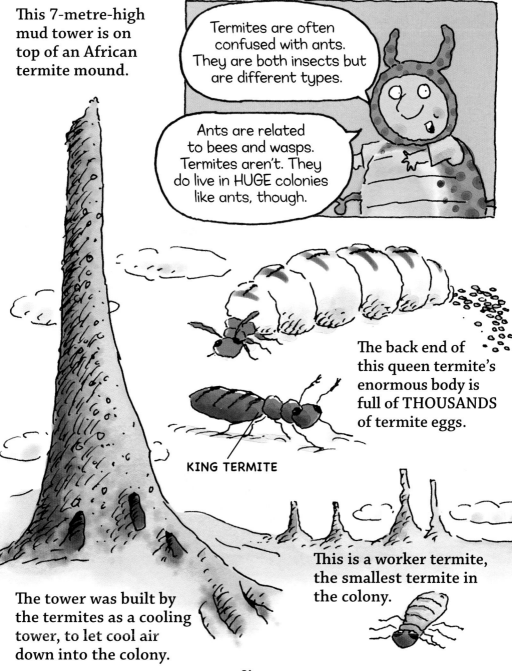

This 7-metre-high mud tower is on top of an African termite mound.

Termites are often confused with ants. They are both insects but are different types.

Ants are related to bees and wasps. Termites aren't. They do live in HUGE colonies like ants, though.

The back end of this queen termite's enormous body is full of THOUSANDS of termite eggs.

KING TERMITE

This is a worker termite, the smallest termite in the colony.

The tower was built by the termites as a cooling tower, to let cool air down into the colony.

Beetle about

The dung beetle rolls dung – animal poo – into a ball.

It uses its back legs to roll the ball to where it wants to bury it.

It uses the dung to feed its babies.

33

Here's another strange-looking insect, Jaggers.

Erch!!!

BANG!

Sorry about that, young Henry! There's been a beetle break-out from my suitcase!

I didn't know you ran a bug ballet now, Mr Bumbo!

BILL BUMBO'S BUG BALLET

Yippee! I'm free!

He does have some crazy ideas!

Beetles have two pairs of wings. The top pair are not for flying. They are like armour, protecting the flying wings hidden under them. Sometimes they are called wing cases.

Now to escape!

WING CASES

SCUTTLE! SCURRY!

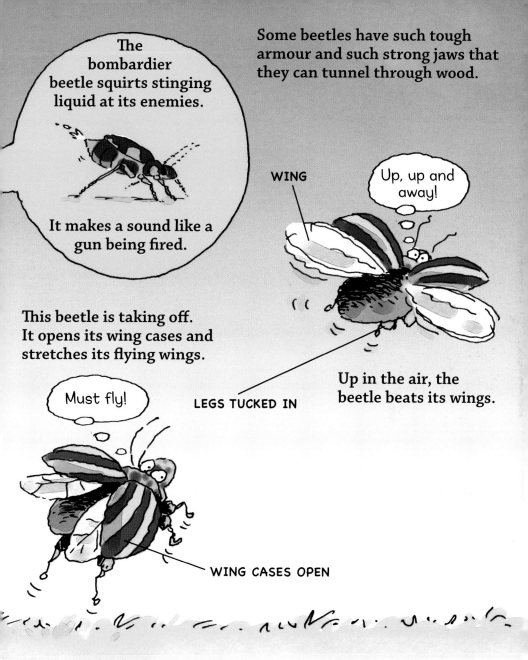

The bombardier beetle squirts stinging liquid at its enemies.

It makes a sound like a gun being fired.

Some beetles have such tough armour and such strong jaws that they can tunnel through wood.

WING

Up, up and away!

This beetle is taking off. It opens its wing cases and stretches its flying wings.

Must fly!

LEGS TUCKED IN

Up in the air, the beetle beats its wings.

WING CASES OPEN

Making a splash

The **pond skater** lives on the surface. Its long legs spread its weight and help it to walk on water.

The **water boatman** "rows" across the water with its back legs.

What most people don't know is that it's lying on its back.

A water boatman taking a dive.

This **water spider** lives underwater but it still needs air to breathe.

Its web is filled with bubbles of air.

36

This **whirligig** lives on the surface too.

It has four eyes: two for looking above the water and two for looking below.

This **diving beetle** eats tadpoles, snails and even small fish.

Saucer bugs are great divers. They collect air through special holes in their bodies.

Young diving beetles look very different. They are called **water tigers**.

Here be dragons!

Look! A dragonfly. They are very fast fliers.

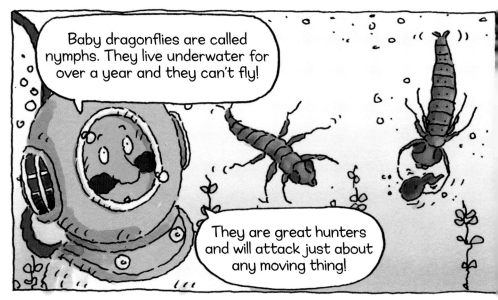

Baby dragonflies are called nymphs. They live underwater for over a year and they can't fly!

They are great hunters and will attack just about any moving thing!

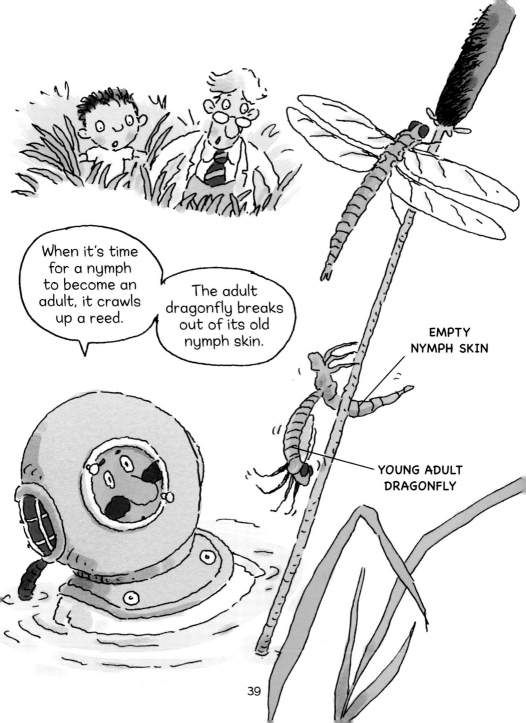

When it's time for a nymph to become an adult, it crawls up a reed.

The adult dragonfly breaks out of its old nymph skin.

EMPTY NYMPH SKIN

YOUNG ADULT DRAGONFLY

A sting in the tail

The scorpion uses its sting to defend itself and to attack.

It curves its tail over its head and STABS with its stinger.

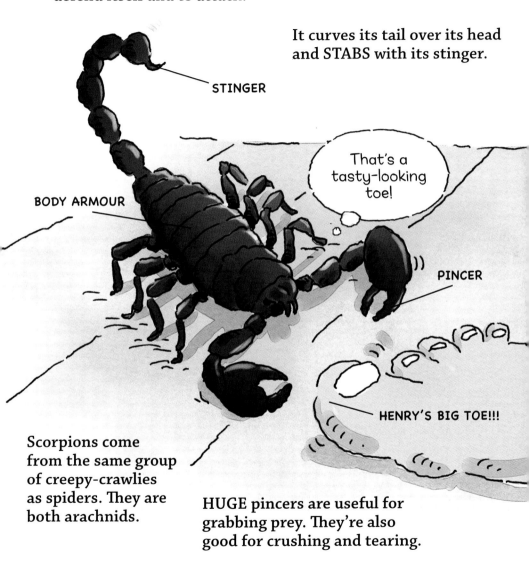

STINGER

BODY ARMOUR

That's a tasty-looking toe!

PINCER

HENRY'S BIG TOE!!!

Scorpions come from the same group of creepy-crawlies as spiders. They are both arachnids.

HUGE pincers are useful for grabbing prey. They're also good for crushing and tearing.

Mummy scorpions carry their babies on their backs for two to four weeks!

Not what they seem

GOTCHA!

PHEW! Thanks, Mr Bumbo. That was close!

Glad you're OK!

Either Henry's shrinking or Big Bug is getting even bigger!

PAT!

Bill is going to have to stay behind until he's rounded up all his escaped – AARGH!

It's me, Hank the Handyman again! How do you like my toadstool costume?

Let me guess. It's camouflage – a disguise – to get even closer to the bugs?

Right! Of course, some creepy-crawlies are also great at pretending to be something else.

This wasp's stripes are a warning: "Stay away. I sting!"

This hover fly can't sting, but it looks like a wasp to fool its enemies!

At first glance, this may look like leaves. Look more closely and you'll find a leaf insect pretending to be one.

This clever disguise is a great way of hiding from birds that might want to eat it!

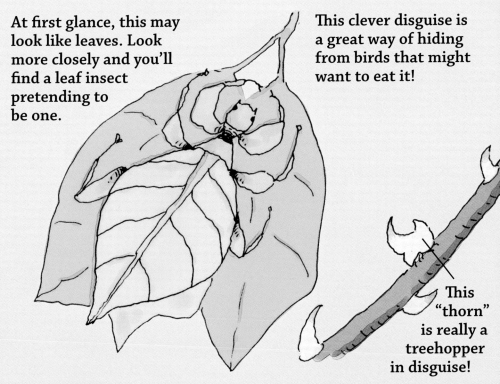

This "thorn" is really a treehopper in disguise!

Scary tricks

Because this mantis looks so like a flower, insects looking for nectar are attracted to it and end up getting eaten!

Hide and seek

You can see how the stick insect got its name. It looks just like one!

This grasshopper blends into the green grass.

It's trying to hide from the birds that might want to eat it.

Wow! So many creepy-crawlies seem to be pretending to be something that they're not! Or just trying to hide to stay alive!

That mantis was CREEPY...

The praying mantis

The praying mantis's claws have jagged edges (a bit like teeth). This is to give the mantis extra grip on its live prey.

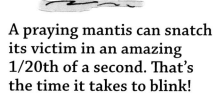

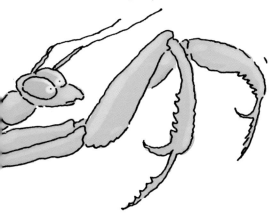

A praying mantis can snatch its victim in an amazing 1/20th of a second. That's the time it takes to blink!

I have a strange feeling I'm being followed.

This praying mantis looks a bit like it's praying with its claws folded together. That's certainly how it gets its name.

It is green to match the leaves.

46

The mantis's claws can unfold amazingly quickly...

... and grab its prey before the poor creature knows what's happening.

Light fright!

All fireflies glow. Grown-up fireflies flash messages at each other.

This grown-up male firefly is flashing his light as he flies above a female. The light is made by a special mixture of chemicals in his bottom.

The female flashes back from the grass below.

Each different type of firefly has its own flashing code.

It is very young fireflies and female fireflies without wings that are called glow worms.

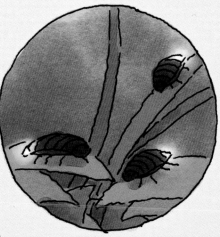

The secret of silk

Silk is made by silkworms. These are caterpillars of the silk moth. They only eat the leaves of the mulberry tree.

Silk farmers collect the leaves and put them in special baskets as food for hundreds of caterpillars living in them.

When the caterpillars are ready to change into grown-ups, they begin to squeeze silk out of holes called spinnerets.

The silkworms then wrap themselves in silk cases. It is from these that people spin silk and make silk cloth.

"Helpful" creepy-crawlies

OK, so silkworms might be handy for humans, but I can't think of any other useful creepy-crawlies.

What about bees for honey?

According to this book, over 500 kinds of creepy-crawlies are regularly eaten by people all over the world.

I've just found this jar of caterpillars in chilli-tomato sauce. They're popular in Africa.

MOPANI WORMS

There's a difference between being useful and being EATEN!

Ladybirds eat the harmful greenfly in our garden.

Most fruit and vegetables (including apples, oranges and onions) need insects to spread their pollen to grow.

Many bugs help to break up the soil, making it just right for plants and crops to grow in.

Creepy-crawlies are often eaten by other animals which, in turn, help humans.

Danger! Danger!

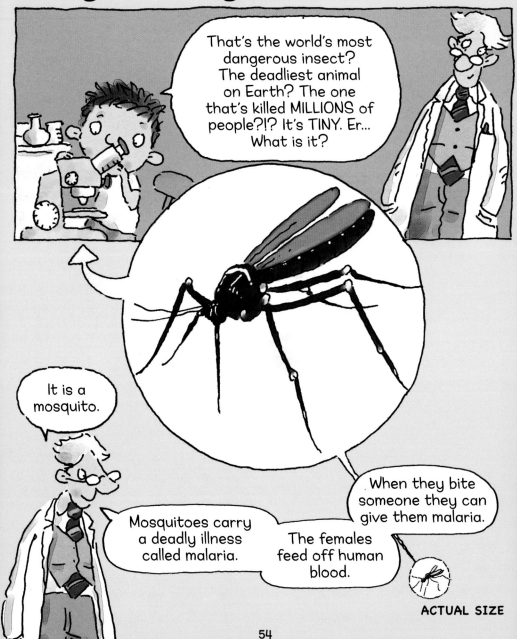

That's the world's most dangerous insect? The deadliest animal on Earth? The one that's killed MILLIONS of people?!? It's TINY. Er... What is it?

It is a mosquito.

When they bite someone they can give them malaria.

Mosquitoes carry a deadly illness called malaria.

The females feed off human blood.

ACTUAL SIZE

WANTED
DEAD OR ALIVE

THE LOCUST

This may look harmless on its own, but a swarm of locusts made up of TENS OF MILLIONS of them eats THOUSANDS OF TONNES of food in a day. This includes people's crops.

THE COCKROACH

Cockroaches are most unwelcome (uninvited) guests in a home. Scuttling over surfaces and feeding on whatever food they can find, they can quickly spread GERMS and DISEASES.

THE FLY

The common housefly is forever spreading GERMS around the house.

THE FLEA

It was fleas from rats that spread the plague across Europe in the 17th century KILLING MILLIONS OF PEOPLE.

Record-breakers!

Those creepy-crawlies may seem bad to us, but they're just trying to stay alive...

It's the fleas I hate!

But we love spending time with you, Mothball!

SCRITCH!

Great news, guys. Mum says I can keep you both!

YIPPEE!

Come and join me, Henry. I think you'll like what you find. Meet the record-breakers!

Some of the world's longest creepy-crawlies are the giant walking sticks. They grow up to 55 cm long.

You should see my dad!

56

The world's w-i-d-e-s-t insect is the Hercules emperor moth. With its wings outstretched, it is the size of a dinner plate!

The heaviest creepy-crawly is the goliath beetle. It weighs as much as a hamster!

The world's smallest insect is probably the fairy fly. It's smaller than the dot on the "i" in its name.

The fastest-running insect is the tropical cockroach. It reaches speeds of over 5 km an hour.

The long-distance flying record goes to the monarch butterfly. Each year, some fly from Canada to Mexico. That's over 3,500 km.

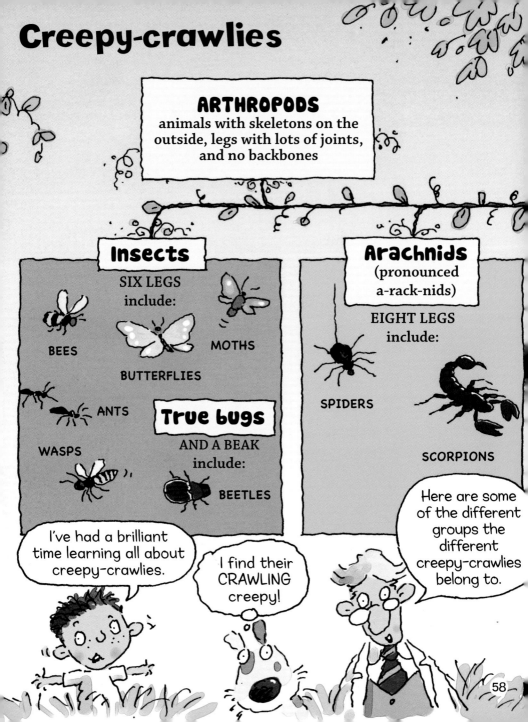

Creepy-crawlies

ARTHROPODS
animals with skeletons on the outside, legs with lots of joints, and no backbones

Insects

SIX LEGS include:

BEES

MOTHS

BUTTERFLIES

ANTS

WASPS

True bugs

AND A BEAK include:

BEETLES

Arachnids
(pronounced a-rack-nids)

EIGHT LEGS include:

SPIDERS

SCORPIONS

I've had a brilliant time learning all about creepy-crawlies.

I find their CRAWLING creepy!

Here are some of the different groups the different creepy-crawlies belong to.

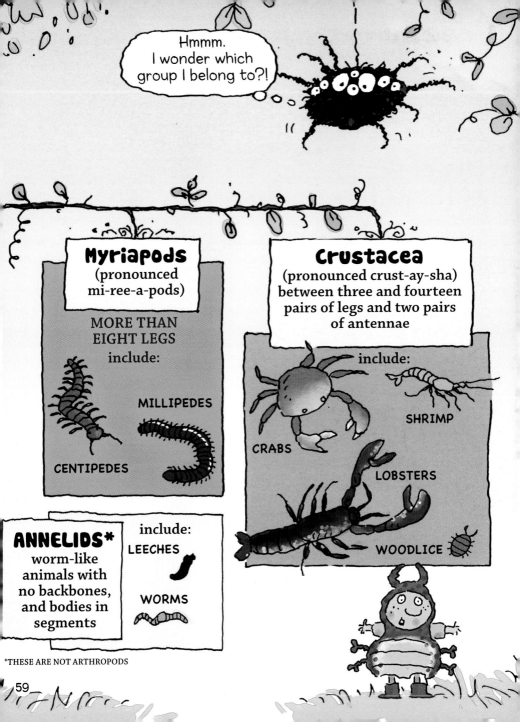

Hmmm. I wonder which group I belong to?!

Myriapods
(pronounced mi-ree-a-pods)

MORE THAN EIGHT LEGS
include:

MILLIPEDES

CENTIPEDES

Crustacea
(pronounced crust-ay-sha) between three and fourteen pairs of legs and two pairs of antennae

include:

CRABS

SHRIMP

LOBSTERS

WOODLICE

ANNELIDS*
worm-like animals with no backbones, and bodies in segments

include:
LEECHES

WORMS

*THESE ARE NOT ARTHROPODS

59

Glossary

Cephalothorax: the joined head-and-thorax part of certain creepy-crawlies such as spiders.

Chrysalis: a moth or butterfly inside a hard shell, at the stage between having been a caterpillar and being an adult.

Colony: a large number of insects living together.

Drone: a type of male bee that has no sting and doesn't make honey.

Dung: a name for animal poo.

Feelers (sometimes called antennae): wire-like, they stick out of the front of an insect's head (usually in twos) and are mainly used for touching and smelling.

Fungus: a type of plant which has no roots, leaves or flowers, such as a toadstool or mushroom.

Germs: microscopic organisms which can cause illness.

Hive: a home made especially for bees by people.

Lens: the part of the eye that focuses light.

Malaria: a disease deadly to humans, carried by female mosquitoes.

Moulting: the shedding of feathers, fur or skin so that new feathers, fur or skin can grow in its place.

Nectar: the sweet-tasting liquid that bees take from flowers to make their honey.

Organisms: living animals and plants.

Pincer: a claw that is particularly good at pinching!

Plague: a serious disease which is quick to spread to lots of people.

Pollen: powdery grains inside flowers, carried by insects and the wind from plant to plant. Without this happening, many new flowers would not grow.

Prey: a creature hunted and eaten by another creature.

Proboscis: a long tube-like body part that some creepy-crawlies use to suck up their food and drink.

Tuffet: a low seat or mound of earth. (So now you know!)

Ultraviolet light: a special kind of light that the human eye cannot see without special equipment.

Index

Henry's House

We hope you enjoyed your visit

to **Henry's House**

Come back soon!

Look out for:
- Bodies
- Egyptians
- Dinosaurs
- Knights and Castles
- Space